A Modern Nerd's Guide to

Renaissance Fairs

BY JILL KEPPELER

Gareth Stevens
PUBLISHING

Please visit our website, www.garethstevens.com. For a free color catalog of all our high-quality books, call toll free 1-800-542-2595 or fax 1-877-542-2596.

Library of Congress Cataloging-in-Publication Data

Names: Keppeler, Jill, author.
Title: A modern nerd's guide to Renaissance fairs / Jill Keppeler.
Other titles: Geek out!
Description: New York : Gareth Stevens, [2020] | Series: Geek out! | Includes
  bibliographical references and index.
Identifiers: LCCN 2019004381| ISBN 9781538240229 (pbk.) | ISBN 9781538240243
  (library bound) | ISBN 9781538240236 (6 pack)
Subjects: LCSH: Renaissance fairs–Juvenile literature. | Role
  playing–Juvenile literature. | Festivals–Juvenile literature. |
  Medievalism–Juvenile literature.
Classification: LCC GT4580 .K47 2020 | DDC 394/.60973–dc23
LC record available at https://lccn.loc.gov/2019004381

First Edition

Published in 2020 by
Gareth Stevens Publishing
111 East 14th Street, Suite 349
New York, NY 10003

Designer: Sarah Liddell
Editor: Abby Badach Doyle

Photo credits: Cover, pp. 1, 25 Boykov/Shutterstock.com; texture used throughout StrelaStudio/Shutterstock.com; p. 5 Frank Romeo/Shutterstock.com; p. 6 John Preito/Contributor/Denver Post/Getty Images; pp. 7, 14 betto rodrigues/Shutterstock.com; p. 8 Education Images/Contributor/Universal Images Group/Getty Images; p. 9 Joe Sohm/Visions of America/Contributor/Universal Images Group/Getty Images; p. 13 picture alliance/Contributor/picture alliance/Getty Images; p. 15 Pierre Jean Durieu/Shutterstock.com; p. 17 Rob Hainer/Shutterstock.com; p. 18 val lawless/Shutterstock.com; p. 19 Milan Ivosevic/Shutterstock.com; p. 20 Lowe Liaguno/Shutterstock.com; p. 21 Waring Abbott/Contributor/Michael Ochs Archives/Getty Images; p. 22 Michael Warwick/Shutterstock.com; p. 23 Anadolu Agency/Contributor/Anadolu Agency/Getty Images; p. 27 Xinhua News Agency/Contributor/Xinhua News Agency/Getty Images.

Printed in the United States of America

CPSIA compliance information: Batch #CS19GS: For further information contact Gareth Stevens, New York, New York at 1-800-542-2595.

CONTENTS

Words in the glossary appear in **bold** type the first time they are used in the text.

A TIME OF LORDS AND LADIES

Do you love to read books about knights and queens and noble quests? Do you like to dress up and pretend to be someone else? Do you like history and music? If so, you might love to visit a Renaissance fair! These events (often called "Ren fairs") are outdoor gatherings that generally offer food, entertainment, and shopping. Ren fairs are often themed around an imaginary account of the 16th century.

If you visit a fair and really like its atmosphere, you might want to go a step further. Many people dress up and become a part of the fun!

PART OF THE STORY!

You don't have to know much about the time period to visit a Renaissance fair. Many people just wear their usual clothes and enjoy the activity going on around them. However, be warned. You still might find yourself pulled into an **impromptu** dance or asked to bow to the queen!

This photo shows the front gates of the New York Renaissance Faire. You don't have to dress up when you attend to have fun. (But it doesn't hurt!)

NEW YORK RENAISSANCE FAIRE

WHERE FANTASY RULES

CLICK AND PRINT

ENTER HERE

The Queen Bids thee welcome

FAIR HISTORY

US Renaissance fairs started in the 1960s in California. Teacher Phyllis Patterson and her husband, Ron, started a children's art and theater program in their backyard in 1963. The programs were very popular. Soon, a Los Angeles radio station asked the Pattersons to help with a fundraiser. The Renaissance Pleasure Faire and May Market was born!

This first fair became a yearly event, and it inspired other fairs throughout the country. Dozens of fairs take place to this day—some for a single day or weekend, others every weekend for months. Some just have tents, while some have sites with actual buildings.

This photo from the 1970s shows people at the Colorado Renaissance festival. The festival takes place in Larkspur, Colorado.

THE FIRST FAIR

The Patterson family no longer runs
the first Renaissance fair takes
not in the same location from
exists today. Now called California.
Renaissance Pleasure Faire visited
place on Saturdays and
April to May near
More than 6 mil
it since it

REALLY RENAISSANCE?

"Renaissance" refers to a time in Europe between **medieval** and modern times. It's usually considered to start in the 14th century in Italy and last until the 17th century. Many fairs are set during the time of Queen Elizabeth I of England, in the 16th century. Some go a little earlier or later.

Some fairs set their location in a **fictional** town. The Sterling Renaissance Festival in Sterling, New York, is set in a pretend town called Warwick, England. (Fun fact: Warwick is also the name of a real English town!) Many fairs don't worry too much about historical **accuracy.** Some use **fantasy** elements and characters!

Many fairs have someone dress up and pretend to be Queen Elizabeth – sometimes young, sometimes older.

ELIZABETH

Elizabeth I was queen of England from 1558 to 1603, starting when she was only 25 years old. This is often called the Elizabethan Age. During this time, England became a major power in many things, including theater, art, and poetry. For many reasons, it's considered a golden age for the country.

CAST OF CHARACTERS

Queen Elizabeth isn't the only "character" you might see at a Renaissance fair. Many fairs also have actors pretending to be other royalty, local lords, townsfolk, and even pirates and jesters. Some have more than one role, or part. For example, musicians often stay in character as a member of the fair's setting even when they're not performing music.

It can be fun to interact with fair characters! Talk to them and ask them questions. Many will have histories for their characters. Don't try to get them to break character, though. That's no fun for anyone! "Breaking character" means to stop acting as the character for some reason.

WHAT'S IN A NAME?

Characters at Renaissance fairs might be from many different social stations. Call people "sir" or "mistress" if you're not sure of their title. However, if you're talking to nobility, you'll want to use "my lord" or "my lady." If you speak to the queen, use "your grace" or "your highness"!

HOW TO SPEAK AT A RENAISSANCE FAIR

- **ANON:** UNTIL LATER
- **AYE:** YES
- **FAREWELL OR FARE THEE WELL:** GOODBYE
- **FIE!:** UGH!
- **HITHER:** HERE
- **HUZZAH!:** HURRAY!
- **GOOD MORROW:** GOOD DAY
- **NAY:** NO
- **PRITHEE:** PLEASE
- **PRIVY:** BATHROOM
- **WELL MET:** HELLO
- **YON:** THERE, OVER THERE

You don't have to speak in Elizabethan language to go to a Renaissance fair, but many people find it fun! You don't have to know everything to use some words and sayings. Here are a few to try.

THE THUNDER OF HOOVES

One highlight of many Renaissance fairs is the joust. These exciting events are often easy to find on the fair grounds—just follow the cheers, the clash of metal, and the sound of hooves pounding the ground!

A joust is a **competition** between two knights and their horses. In a joust, a knight-and-horse pair charges at the other at high speed. Each knight tries to hit their **opponent** with a lance and knock him to the ground. Once the knights are on the ground, they might battle with their swords, too! People watching take sides and cheer on their favorite knight.

KNIGHT TIME

Like many other activities at Renaissance fairs, jousts have their roots in the real world. These mock battles took place at European tournaments, which were events in which knights competed with each other with their fighting skills. The **tradition** of jousting ended around the beginning of the 16th century.

Renaissance festival knights aren't in as much danger as knights from medieval times, but their job still takes a lot of training!

PIPES ON THE WIND

Music is a big part of many Renaissance festivals. If you check the fair event listings, you're likely to find musicians and musical groups that perform at particular times and places. Look for wandering performers who may break into impromptu performances around the grounds!

Fair music may include groups with **authentic** instruments performing real music written during the Renaissance period. Some fairs include groups with more modern music and instruments as well! Renaissance fairs may feature **Celtic** music, traditional English music, **maritime** music, or music from other traditions. Keep your ears open and ask questions, and you might learn a lot!

These musicians are performing at a Renaissance fair. Do any of their instruments look different to you?

STRANGER SOUNDS

Some of the performers you'll see may be playing familiar instruments, such as guitars, fiddles, and flutes. However, there may be some different instruments, too! You might see someone playing a bodhran (BOW-rahn), which is a flat, handheld drum; different types of bagpipes; or a gemshorn, a type of pipe made from a cow's horn.

THE WORLD'S A STAGE

In addition to wandering characters, jousts, and music, you can see many other types of shows at a Renaissance fair. There are some you might expect—jugglers and dancers, magicians and funny acts—but some might surprise you. Some fairs have their own acting troupes, or groups, that provide shows in a fair theater or wherever characters might interact . . . even in a mud pit!

Have you ever heard of a sword swallower? At a Renaissance fair, you might see one! Fairs may also host fire eaters. These performers pretend to swallow swords or eat fire . . . or do they really do it?

JUST FOR KIDS

Many times, there are events at Ren fairs that are just for kids. You might be able to be knighted by the queen or have tea with her! You might have a chance to take sword lessons or go on a quest to find something in the fair.

You never know what you might see at a Renaissance fair!

WORKS OF ART

Shopping might not sound like a lot of fun—but you can find cool things for sale at a Renaissance fair that you might not be able to find anywhere else. Sometimes you can buy glass bowls or cups that you just watched a glassblower create, or real swords like something a knight would carry. (Your parents might not agree with that last idea, but it can still be fun to look!)

There often are smaller things for sale, too. You might find some homemade soap, a stuffed animal, or even a little hand-bound book you can write in.

Some artists at Ren fairs make their creations right in front of you!

TURKEY LEGS AND PIZZA PYES

The classic Ren fair food item is a big turkey leg that you eat with your hands! There are also meat pies and kebabs, which are chunks of food cooked on a stick. You can also find foods that probably aren't all that authentic, such as "pizza pyes."

DRESS THE PART

If you want to take part in a Ren fair a little more, you can dress up! Looking at items for sale from fair artisans, or arts and crafts makers, is a good place to start. You don't have to go right from street clothes to full fair garb, or clothing. Maybe start with a crown of flowers for your hair or a toy sword to carry at your side.

If you have longer hair, many fairs offer hair-braiding services that can make you fit right in. Some fairs rent costumes if you want to try one out. An old Halloween costume could work, too.

People get their hair braided at this booth at the New York Renaissance Faire. This can be an easy way to try out a little bit of the fair!

FAIR THEMES

Ren fairs often have themed weekends, during which all the usual fair fun goes on but with an additional theme as well. Common themes are pirates, magic and fairies, kids, Scottish or Celtic, marketplace, time travelers, or heroes. Each day of a weekend might have a different theme, too.

If you want your own fair outfit, there are a few ways to buy or make one. You can buy a full set of clothing at the fair or at an online store that sells Renaissance outfits . . . but this can cost a lot of money, especially for a beginner.

If you can sew or know someone who does, you can find patterns for Renaissance clothing. Or, you can look at secondhand stores, which sell used clothing, to find basic pieces. Then, change the pieces until you like how they look. Start simple! Your basic pieces should be skirts or pants, a shirt with long, full sleeves, and a vest.

Some fairgoers find metal or clay cups at secondhand stores to carry with them. That way, they don't have to drink out of plastic or paper cups and spoil their look!

WHAT TO WEAR

A boy's Renaissance outfit might include boots, pants, a shirt, a vest, and a hat. A girl's outfit might include skirts, a shirt, shoes, and a bodice, which is the upper part of the dress. However, if you want to adapt your outfit to make it your own, go for it!

FANTASY AND HISTORY

Although Renaissance fairs are inspired by real history, many embrace fantasy elements, too! You may see people dressed as fairies, pixies, elves, or other make-believe creatures. This can be a fun way to use your imagination and see what you can think up.

However, before you dress up to go to a Ren fair, always check the fair's rules. Some may have rules to keep things authentic, or historically correct. If you carry a sword or another weapon with your costume, you may need to have it peace tied. This means the weapon is tied in its holder so it can't be removed. Some fairs ban all weapons.

HUMAN POWER!

Sometimes, Ren fairs have rides—but they're not the kind you can find at your average carnival. Ren fair rides tend to be human powered! Fair workers may whip you around on a dragon-shaped swing or spin you around in a giant barrel. Sometimes there are games, too.

fairies are a popular fantasy costume you might see at a Ren fair. How would you want to dress up for your first fair?

ENJOY THE JOURNEY

Today, more than 50 years after the first Ren fair in California, there are dozens of fairs in the United States. They're all a little different, but that's part of the fun!

The Texas Renaissance Festival is one of the biggest in the country and has a King's Feast as part of its events. At the Minnesota Renaissance Festival, you can bring your dog to Pet Fest or run the Turkey Leg Trot 5K. The New York Renaissance Faire, located in Tuxedo, New York, features Robin Hood and his merry band as part of its story. What can you find out about your local festival?

THE FAIR CIRCUIT

You might see some names in common at Ren fairs, even fairs that are across the country from each other. Some actors and artists go from fair to fair all year. The act of Don Juan and Miguel, for example, performs at a handful of fairs throughout the United States, from Texas to New York!

The Texas Renaissance festival in Todd Mission, Texas, has been taking place for more than 45 years.

Water & Soda

BIRD Whistles

GO YE FORTH!

Do you still want to learn more about Renaissance fairs? The best way to do that is to go to one and talk to people! Ask questions and listen to the answers. Try out your Elizabethan words. No one will laugh at you if your words aren't perfect. Speak slowly and do your best.

You can take part in all the activities you see at a fair, or you can just wander around and soak up the atmosphere. There's no one right way to go to a Renaissance fair. Just be curious, make sure you're comfortable if you wear a costume, and have fun!

THINGS TO TAKE TO A FAIR

Renaissance fairs are generally outside. Make sure you have sunscreen and perhaps a jacket to help you stay warm and dry. It's good to bring cash, because not all artists or sellers will take credit cards. A reusable shopping bag to carry special purchases is a good idea, too!

TALK LIKE A RENNIE!

RENNIE: SOMEONE WHO SPENDS A LOT OF TIME AT A RENAISSANCE FAIR, EITHER AS AN EMPLOYEE OR A VISITOR.

BAF: STANDS FOR "BASIC FAIR ACCENT." THIS IS A SORT OF BRITISH ACCENT, OR WAY OF PRONOUNCING WORDS, USED AT REN FAIRS. IT'S BASED ON ELIZABETHAN LANGUAGE, NOT MODERN BRITISH ACCENTS.

PLAYTRON: A COMBINATION OF "**PATRON**" AND "PLAYER." THESE AREN'T EMPLOYEES, BUT THEY'RE PEOPLE WHO DRESS UP TO VISIT THE FAIR AND DO SO A LOT.

PUSH MONKEY: FAIR EMPLOYEES WHO MAKE THE RIDES WORK.

MUNDANE: A FAIR VISITOR WHO WEARS REGULAR CLOTHES.

If you're around a Renaissance fair long enough, you might start to learn some of the language longtime fairgoers and performers use—and not just Elizabethan language!

29

GLOSSARY

accuracy: freedom from mistakes

authentic: made the same way as the original

Celtic: related to the Celts, a people who lived in ancient Britain and parts of western Europe

competition: an event in which people try to win

fantasy: something produced by the imagination

fictional: something that is made up or not real

impromptu: not prepared ahead of time, done without preparation

maritime: relating to the sea or sailing

medieval: having to do with the Middle Ages, a time in European history from about 500 to 1500

opponent: the person or team you must beat to win a game

patron: a person who buys goods or uses services

tradition: a long-practiced custom

FOR MORE INFORMATION

BOOKS

Eding, June. *Who Was Queen Elizabeth?* New York, NY: Penguin Workshop, 2017.

Nelson, Kristen Rajczak. *Renaissance Fairs: Role-Playing for Fun and Profit.* New York, NY: Rosen Publishing, 2016.

Roman, Carole P. *If You Were Me and Lived In...Elizabethan England: An Introduction to Civilizations Throughout Time.* Andover, MA: Chelshire, 2017.

WEBSITES

Cheap and Easy Costumes
www.ccrenfaire.com/renaissance-costume-shop/cheap-easy-costumes
The Central Coast Renaissance Festival website provides tips on putting together a quick and inexpensive costume to wear to a Ren fair.

The Original Renaissance Pleasure Faire
www.renfair.com/socal/
Learn about the Ren fair that started it all and continues to this day, including a page on fair history.

Welcome to the Renaissance Faire
www.renfaire.com/
This website offers a lot of information on what a Renaissance fair is and how to fit in at one, including tips on a fair accent.